REBELLIOU$ WEALTH

HOW TO BREAK THE RULES (NOT THE LAWS) TO CREATE YOUR OWN ECONOMY

Ray Bolden

ISBN-13: 978-0692418789 (Bold Ambition Worldwide, LLC)
ISBN-10: 0692418784

Dedication

This is dedicated to the people who want to challenge authority and live unconventional, remarkable lives!

Acknowledgements

I want to give special acknowledgement to my wife Karen and my sons Raymond and Don for their reviews, critiques, suggestions and unwavering support.

I also want to recognize and acknowledge my immediate and extended families for their support, encouragement and endless discussions that helped me analyze the complex issues discussed in this book.

Table of Contents

Preface 9

Why Aren't You Rich? 15

Chapter 1

Gun-To-The Head Enlightenment 21

Chapter 2

Heads I Win Tails I Don't Lose 29

Chapter 3

The American Dream...A Love Story 37

Chapter 4

CEO Status Despite The Lack Of

An Advanced Degree 45

Chapter 5

The Last Man Standing 55

Chapter 6

The Successful, The Powerful,

The Accomplished.. 63

Preface

Let me let you in on a little secret: The only person who cares about your personal fulfillment and financial security is you. Do you really think that you're going to save your way to a comfortable retirement working for someone else? I used to think that standard education and my secure military employment were the ticket to both my money and my security, but I challenged traditional assumptions about education, life and work and discovered new solutions that allowed me to shift the balance of power. I learned that it was okay to put my own life ahead of climbing the military ladder and designed my life around what was important to me by defining success for myself.

REBELLIOU$ WEALTH is all about designing the lifestyle you want; allowing you the freedom and income to live the life you long for. Throughout this course, I'm going to share with you my principles of self-reliance and teach you the revolutionary business methods, techniques and strategies that you can use to launch an (information) business that you can run from your home office or wherever you desire with little or no start-up capital or technical expertise. My objective is to inspire you and show you how to stop dreaming about a better life and start living it. I'm going to show you how to redesign your life around your own economic empowerment and interests and combine automated online marketing and outsourcing to build an ethical and lucrative business all while working less and setting your own hours. The lessons I learned in life and business are my greatest asset and my greatest legacy. Through my own experience and personal stories, I'm going to describe exactly how I created my businesses and how you can duplicate my success. I'd like to help you find the courage to redefine success on your own terms and allow you to rebalance your life to achieve the goals most important to you. I created this course to help you do just that. Before you start, there are two points I want to cover. First, I created this course for believers not cynics. This course does not present some 'pie in the sky', 'get rich quick 'scheme. Instead it presents proven strategies for success. The idea is that it's not good to do something stupid even if everybody else is doing it. The logic is, think for yourself instead of following the crowd. I created this course to help bring the message of make your own decisions and live your own life. You can rewrite the rules but it all begins with the deliberate choice to think differently. The purpose of this course is to transform your thinking about life and work. You'll benefit from the transition if you're in a season of life where you're ready to make some changes. If you're feeling stuck in something and have always believed "there must be more to life", this course is for you. Change your thinking to focus first on your goal of living better, however you define that personally.

I don't want to waste your time so to make this course useful to you, you must be open to new ideas, you must be dissatisfied with the status quo, you must be willing to take responsibility and you must be willing to work hard. As you set out on your journey, we'll look at how to identify who you are, redesign your attitude for success and build a business around your unique personal experience so that you can help others solve similar problems in their own lives. We'll also discuss the revolutionary principles behind the success of the *BAD BOYS FINI$H RICH* lifestyle from my previous book and create an action plan for implementing the *REBELLIOU$ WEALTH* strategies within by choosing the right niche business model so you can get started creating your own economy. Again, I'm not talking about a get-rich-quick strategy. *REBELLIOU$ WEALTH* is the manifesto of a movement focused on attitude and lifestyle. This is how I define the term *REBELLIOU$ WEALTH*: Creative self-employment, self-reliance and unconventional lifestyle businesses. Some of these topics will require more study for full mastery but this course is meant to be compact and complete. By applying the lessons within, you'll be fully equipped to accomplish anything you set out to do. I challenge you to do more than you thought possible and if you make some big changes as a result of the ideas you see here, we will both have succeeded. In the event we succeed, you will have the ability and the obligation to live life on your own terms and help other people while you're at it. Nothing will ever be the same. Before we go any

10

further, I like to keep the bullshit and the mediocrity to a minimum so there is no hidden agenda here. Let me save you some time and tell you up front that my motivation is to help people challenge authority and live unconventional, remarkable lives. The mission is to support a full scale revolution with a simple underlying message: You don't have to live your life the way other people expect you to.

Rebellious

Function:

Adjective

1. Defying or resisting established authority or tradition.
2. A desire to resist control or convention.
3. Resistance to an established ruler.
4. Not easily handled or kept in place.
5. Always wanting to go "against the grain" and be different from everyone else.
6. Daring to be different, stand up for what you believe is right & never quit!

.

REBELLIOU$ WEALTH!

"Who else but me?"

~ Puff Daddy
Bad Boys For Life (2001)

Introduction

WHY AREN'T YOU RICH?

During an interview for his book *The Wealth Choice*, John H. Johnson founder and chief executive officer of Ebony magazine asked author Dennis Kimbro, "Why aren't you rich?" "Why aren't you wealthy?" Sitting motionless, Mr. Kimbro was caught off guard because he had never considered the question and he felt ashamed because he couldn't answer the question.

So how do these questions make you feel? Did you sit back in your chair with your hands clasped behind your head and put your feet on your desk because these questions don't apply to you or like Mr. Kimbro, do you feel ashamed because you've wasted time, your talents and your potential? For most people, it's the latter. In contrast, you already have a good idea of how wealthy people, athletes, entertainers and real estate tycoons make millions joyfully every year, so there are only two reasons why you don't have what you want right now: either you don't know the ABC's of making your dreams come true, or if you do, you won't get off the couch to take consistent action on a regular basis. Your problem is that you have spent your entire life thinking that there are rules that you have to follow to be self-reliant. You are wrong!

It can be argued that the great education system in America teaches us to live according to the middle-class way of thinking. We are encouraged to be only as good as our classmates and to subscribe to an average/normal life of reasoning. We are taught that everything is difficult and that other people run our lives. It is expected that our actions, at any particular age, can be analyzed and categorized in such a way that we follow the norm. The bottom line is that we are all expected to be fairly predictable in nature. Personally, for as long as I can remember, I've wanted to do more than just live an average life. I've wanted to have an impact on the world. I have a genuine, heart-felt desire to empower people, to raise them to a higher level of existence.

I've written several books. My latest one called *BAD BOYS FINI$H RICH* is about my own personal entrepreneurial education. In it, I made a dramatic point about the different ways people think about self-reliance and the goals they set. If you have not read this book, I strongly recommend you read it, even before finishing this book. From here on, the lessons in this book will assume you have already read *BAD BOYS FINI$H RICH*. It's a simple book with deep lessons and I believe you will find even deeper insights hidden in the original book once you have finished this book.

WHO ELSE BUT YOU?

In the quote that precedes this chapter, Puffy makes a bold statement: "Who else but me?" For me, it's as if he is saying how dare you think it could be anybody else but me. I have the ambition and the balls to go for mine so, "Who else but me?" So what better time than now to ask, who else but you? Do you want to be the person sitting at the table offering the job or the person sitting at the table asking for a job? We can find the answer, but it requires that you join in a walk on the wild side of self-reliance. This book will give you the courage and understanding you need to feel confident about taking charge of your financial life, whether that means starting your own business or just being more self-reliant, but it only makes sense if you want to take control of your life and your circumstances. This is a fundamental choice that belongs exclusively to you.

Now success in life is more than financial success and positive thinking alone is worthless. *REBELLIOU$ WEALTH* is all about making radical adjustments to the way you think and act that make it easier to create the economy you want, faster and easier than you can imagine. WARNING: When I say radical changes in beliefs and behavior, I mean it. A lot of what you read is going to be hard to swallow. You will be tempted to instantly reject it. You will find it contrary and challenging to what you've been taught and what you believe. It will make you feel uncomfortable, but I have never been concerned with who I may offend and I'm not about to start worrying about it now. This is the truth about how to create your own economy as I know it. To avoid having wasted the price of this book and more importantly to avoid missing out on incredible opportunities to transform your life for the better, you need to tolerate some of the discomfort, to patiently and carefully consider ideas and suggestions that at first seem dead wrong, illogical, irrational and unreasonable to you. If my ideas didn't contradict, conflict and challenge those in your present belief system, something would be wrong!

I fully realize that you may be successful in your own right, but no matter how successful you may be, you will find some ideas in this book that will surprise you, shock you, challenge you, liberate you and benefit you. Contrary to popular belief, you are here because you believe that there is more to you than what others see, but right now you are stuck with the decision to move ahead or stay stuck where you are. The truth is: you've never been comfortable being mediocre; it's not your natural state. You are a *REBELLIOUS WEALTH* seeker, a bad boy or bad girl who finishes rich. The money may not have been deposited into your bank account yet, but it's still who you are. Don't wait for the world's validation.

So to quote Andy Dufresne from the movie The Shawshank Redemption, "Get busy living, or get busy dying!" To encourage you, I'm going to briefly describe my qualifications, to convince you that I am a person that you should take seriously, even though I'm presenting ideas that you may find difficult to accept. I started out in life broke; no resources and I don't have a college degree.

I'm self-educated. I've read more books than most people see in a life time. Principally self-trained, my university was the public library, audio books, bookstore and the school of hard-knocks. By virtue of being regarded as disassociated from the group, and not a team player, little did I know that my desperate rebellion to mediocrity would lead to writing books that point out the beauty of being rebellious and the freedom it can provide. I've found that most people simply want to feel more in control of their lives and have their world make more sense.

Because this isn't a mystery novel here are four points about how acquiring *REBELLIOU$ WEALTH* will impact you personally:

1. You will undergo an elementary yet fundamental shift in perspective because the underlying message is that you can write, direct, produce and star in your own path to wealth.

2. Deep down you will know the truth because you'll know how to deal with business and won't let the critics fuck with you.

3. You will be able to better define your targets and keep moving efficiently toward them because you will understand how to create your own system and not be enslaved by another man's.

4. There will be no turning back because you'll understand that there is a big difference between being in charge and being in control.

In all probability, it will be the best investment of time you will ever make. At the end of each chapter I've placed real-life examples to illustrate various aspects of the new approach. Some relate to the previous chapter, some don't. The examples will remind you that a mandatory element of the method is to view your world from a new perspective. So what are you gonna do? Make a commitment today to apply and master the habits of *REBELLIOU$ WEALTH* seekers described in this course and you'll be ready to use the *REBELLIOU$ WEALTH* strategies I'm going to share with you. Once you get accustomed to living in a more effective, more powerful and passionate way, I promise, you will never go back to your old life.

REBELLIOU$ WEALTH!

"I was pulled this way and that for longer than I can remember. And my problem was that I always tried to go in everyone's way but my own. I have also been called one thing and then another while no one really wished to hear what I called myself. So after years of trying to adopt the opinions of others I finally rebelled. I am an invisible man!"

~ Ralph Ellison, Invisible Man

Chapter One

GUN-TO-THE-HEAD ENLIGHTENMENT

(Become your own genie that you let out of the bottle!)

For many, hearing the old adage "To get want you want, you have to be rebellious", evokes the knee-jerk response that being rebellious is a bad thing. They counter that you should relax and go with the flow, stay loose and not worry much about details. It's my contention that being rebellious and being in control of our lives is mandatory if we are to find peace, success and happiness. In America, you have almost no power if you don't own something. There is no pride in a platform on which you sit if it can be taken away from you in a moment's notice. If you're always waiting for someone else to feed you, you are typically an inch or two away from starvation. You have been seduced into believing that you don't have any real power. That you have to earn it or it has to be given to you, when the truth is, you have more power than you think you do. Either you are in charge of your own destiny or you're not in charge. On that point you have to be clear; you are either free or you are a slave.

What about the generally accepted notion that the person who is rebellious and wants to take control of their lives is someone who needs to loosen up? I submit that that ubiquitous generalization is wrong. I learned that wealth or happiness would not be found in others who have control over me or the way that I think. It would be found in the firm grasp of systemized rebellion. We bask in wealth all around us that has never been seen before but wonder why we are unsatisfied. So we point fingers and complain about our dissatisfaction. There are an infinite number of puzzle pieces out there and for each of us to get what we want in our lives, it's just a matter of seeing those pieces, making a proper selection and then assembling them the way we want so that we are not swayed by peers or public opinion.

REBELLIOU$ WEALTH seekers don't just rail against the system, they strive to become the system and take over the system. I realized that I had to start clearing my mind of the mediocre thoughts that were holding me captive. I started asking, "How can I create more wealth?" and as I did, I began to see a big difference between *REBELLIOU$ WEALTH* seekers and everybody else. Unfortunately, many believe that there is a barrier that keeps them from succeeding, yet if they would learn to use the laws of self-reliance, concentration and action, they would realize that there is a world of opportunity right in front of them.

THE PSYCHOLOGY OF REBELLIOU$
WEALTH HIDDEN IN PLAIN VIEW

Your subconscious mind will produce exactly what you tell it to and most people are playing a small game and produce small results. As well, there is a big difference between a person whose dreams remain just dreams and someone who gets things done. To take it even further, aiming for a goal is totally different than executing a plan. To obtain *REBELLIOU$ WEALTH, BAD BOYS* who *FINI$H RICH* confidently make up their own minds about things and then consistently apply that certainty to the real world. What is stopping you from getting what you want? Who you are always determines what you get. Something about you and something that you consistently do is stopping you from living the life you deserve. What personal habit is standing in your way? If you can't figure this out, you are in denial. Take heed to the words of Terrance Howard as Coach Jim Ellis in the movie Pride, "You are your own worst enemy. You got so much potential but you ain't gone do none of it because you won't get out of your own way!" Whatever you envision right now, whatever you aspire to at this moment, you already have some of the elements at hand. Take the first step and the next step will become clear. The problem is, everybody wants to play in everybody else's sandbox, sacrificing their very identities to their detriment. That's the magic behind *REBELLIOU$ WEALTH*. People may not always think big of themselves, but they get very excited by those who do. So ask yourself what would a bad boy who finishes rich do right now? Then take action like the *REBELLIOU$ WEALTH* seeker that you are.

In his book, *Why We Do What We Do: Understanding Self-Motivation,* Edward L. Deci writes: Rather than waiting for the world to give them what they want, people can become more proactive in making things happen for themselves. They can get the interactive process working on their behalf by behaving more autonomously. Their personality and the social contexts in which they operate are synergistic and together they affect people's experiences and actions. If financial success remains a mystery to you, it might be because the wealth creation process does not in any way resemble your notion of steady progress. First you have to be willing to accept that changing your behavior and following through on a few everyday practices can bring you financial success that you may have only dreamed of. So what does this really mean? To me, it says that the principles of *REBELLIOU$ WEALTH* will provide the best and most attractive new route to affluence for any intelligent, educated person willing to practice them. Why? Because we get to do what every kid dreams about: Rethink preconceived beliefs and habits and be willing to question the received wisdom we have long relied upon. It's time to unleash the *REBELLIOU$ WEALTH* within you because let's be honest, most people aren't on track to become millionaires anyway. The truth is, only your beliefs and behaviors separate you from the affluent. It's time to reverse-engineer the rules. Why? Because we count on institutions to provide us with social stability and rules to live by, but it's obvious that the rules are all broken. You know it and I know it. If you play by the rules today, without your own game within the game; you're probably going to end up broke.

If you are like I used to be, you probably thought that your job was a ticket to both money and security. Unfortunately, employment without a *REBELLIOU$ WEALTH* plan can be more of an income for dummies plan than a lifetime meal ticket because you are required to contribute most of your waking hours to the bottom line, but that's no longer a guarantee for steady pay, job security, decent health coverage and a comfortable retirement. *REBELLIOU$ WEALTH* allows you to enjoy financial independence, creative control and schedule flexibility traditionally only available to people who already have millions in the bank. But the money is not the point. Your lifestyle as the owner is. I want to help you develop a new attitude and mindset that grows into a satisfying ongoing lifestyle, so like it's predecessor, *BAD BOYS FINI$H RICH, REBELLIOU$ WEALTH* is a habit and an attitude! The goal is to find a *REBELLIOU$ WEALTH* attitude balance that is comfortable and fulfilling for you.

People seek riches, not for the sake of being rich, but to be happy. If you want to be happy, you have to put your life in sync with your deepest values and beliefs. Now I know this isn't an easy thing to do, particularly in western society where we are subject to so many outside influences. It's too easy to get intoxicated with the dream of what conventional success is going to do for your happiness, yet conventional success and happiness are two entirely different things. Since you have read this far, at this very moment, you're probably having what is for you is a natural reaction to feeling controlled. The reason for this is that your attitude and the actions you choose to take help create the social context in which you live. Take heed to the words of Enrich Fromm from his book Escape from Freedom: "Modern man lives under the illusion that he knows what he wants, while he actually wants what he is supposed to want. Indeed, in today's consumer society, advertisers and the media dictate what people are supposed to want. Many people consume this programming greedily instead of stopping to question what will truly make them happy. After all, it is much easier to try to fit in with the majority than to question what the majority is doing." Don't buy into the sentimental notion that being rebellious is an absurd, erratic thing and that success is only attainable by a few of the extremely talented. You have to break out. You are here because at some point you have been told that you weren't good enough or that you weren't a team player because your values didn't line up with the masses. So you have to convince yourself that your limits are smaller and fewer than the imaginary ones you have been subjecting yourself to.

As a student of *Bold Ambition*, we are all free agents now. We are all entrepreneurs, whether we want to be or not. We don't have to impress you, we don't have to be influenced by you and in our own creative way, we are going to show you by being true to our own identity and not being second or consumer to anyone. The bottom line is that many people don't play by the same rules as you and I respect the fact that people have a right to live their own lives the way they choose, but there is no obligation on your part to apologize to anyone for enjoying your life. *REBELLIOU$ WEALTH* is a process of self-development, self-discovery and self-love. Stop caring what others think of you. Your duty is always to yourself. Looking out for number one is important because you have to take care of yourself if you want to take care of your family. As long as your lifestyle isn't illegal or harmful to anybody, FUCK EM! When you are truly successful in this game called *REBELLIOU$ WEALTH*, you don't have anything to prove to anyone. There comes a time when you must get your shit together and show the world and yourself what you can do and today is that day.

"REBELLIOU$ WEALTH" – EXERCISE APPENDIX-A

There is an old saying, "ask the right questions and you'll get the right answers" so sit undisturbed for a minute or so, and really think deeply about the following questions. Now we both know you'll probably scan the questions before answering them, but that's okay, the ones that need to stand out to you will show themselves. All the questions are internally driven so there are no external factors involved in trying to improve these areas of your life… it's all you. Once you are clear about who you really are, your life would improve dramatically. This will improve your confidence, your competence, and your determination to live by your values.

- What kind of things have you done which others have described as "outstanding?"

- Do you live your life according to your beliefs and values or do you stray from them when things get a little tough?

- What things do you believe you do better than most people around you?

- Do you listen to others before putting your own values first?

- How true to your beliefs and values do you live your life?

- How confident are you as a person?

- How expressive are you about your thoughts, feelings and life plans?

- Are you living your life or having a life?

- What makes you special, unique and talented?

- Do you stand for what you believe in or are you pleasing others?

- Who's permission are you waiting on to achieve your goals?

REBELLIOU$ WEALTH!

"Who the fuck you think you fucking with… I'm the fucking boss!"

~ Rick Ross, Hustlin

Chapter Two

HEADS I WIN, TAILS I DON'T LOSE

(Always set yourself up to win)

There is, right now, this minute, more disposable income by any measurement, dollars, percentages, ratios, you pick the statistics you like, than ever before. On top of that, new categories of products and services, new industries and new opportunities abound. Stop and think about all of the businesses that exist now that didn't exist before and marvel at it all. It seems that everyday somebody invents another new means of attracting wealth. I am absolutely convinced that if you don't do well financially in America today, it is either due to utter ignorance of opportunity or choice. It definitely is not due to lack of opportunity. If you don't share these beliefs, if you doubt and question the fact of unlimited readily available abundance of both opportunity and money, then you need to invest time and energy on your own fact finding research mission and make this sale to yourself.

I listen to people and watch them closely, to try to determine the extent and depth of their wealth drive or lack thereof. Personally, every single day, I choose to compete. I compete against the odds. The more aware you make your mind, conscious and subconscious of just how much affluence there is, just how much money is moving around, the more easily you will attract wealth. We're making this up you know? All of it. Whatever life you're living is the product of your beliefs, conditioning and imagination. You're choosing it. If it's not as wonderful as you would like it to be, you have some choices. You can accept it. You can blame somebody else for it or you can create it and work hard as hell to make it the way that you want it to be.

31

The truth, known to all *BAD BOYS* who *FINI$H RICH* is: *REBELLIOU$ WEALTH* creation and attraction requires a willingness to risk and experience failure and emotional resiliency and to recover from it quickly, decisively, passionately and persistently. This means that taking 100% responsibility for your life means you acknowledge that you create everything that happens to you. It means you understand that you are the cause of all you experience. If you want to be truly successful and I know you do, then you will have to give up blaming and complaining and take total responsibility for your life. That means all of your results, your successes and your failures.

But contrary to what some think, *REBELLIOU$ WEALTH* doesn't happen in a sudden burst of inspiration; it is a disciplined process that achieves results by focusing on a specific outcome. This is the struggle for your own freedom, so ask yourself, what is powerful, productive and positive and can lead me toward what I want? Then do it now! Make it an obsession and let it become your reality before the world even thinks it is a possibility. But there's more to the story than passion and drive. I know from personal experience that self-reliance and entrepreneurship are tools that can create great wealth and personal enrichment in your life and this chapter clarifies any misconceptions that you may have about your ability to succeed. So before you go any further, I want to tell you a story that demonstrates exactly how you can make *REBELLIOU$ WEALTH* a reality.

SOLVING ALL OF YOUR MONEY PROBLEMS WITH THE STROKE OF A PEN

The worst stress and frustration I ever experienced was working for someone else, accepting a nominal salary, putting up with corporate political nonsense and lacking the personal freedom to pursue my own innovative, value creating ideas. For those of you who read *BAD BOYS FINI$H RICH*, you know my story of receiving a business opportunity magazine in the mail addressed to the former homeowner. I flipped through it and my curiosity got the best of me. I paid particular interest to an ad about a guy who made $100,000.00 creating little books and selling them from home. I ordered it and studied it over and over again. Shortly thereafter, I created my own little books and began selling them through the mail. The response was slow, but I continued to follow the tips, tricks and techniques that I learned from his system and sales trickled in. This was enough to get me excited. I started doing research and gained ideas at the bookstore, library and by listening to audio programs. I took those ideas and with a lot of trial and error, developed my own winning formula and with a little ingenuity and creativity, I adapted this formula to the Internet.

It can be misconstrued that I stumbled upon my fortune by sheer accident, but I get a vision in my head and feel compelled to make it real so I rewrote history so that it looked like it had been my plan all along. I am driven by a quote from Frank Costello (Jack Nicholson) from the movie The Departed, "I don't want to be a product of my environment. I want my environment to be a product of me", and this experience allowed me to invent who Ray Bolden was going to become. No one was coming to save me; so I had to save myself and it was through this internal struggle that the *BAD BOYS FIN$H RICH* brand was born and I created a lifestyle around it.

WHERE THINKING AND COMMERCE MEET

Entrepreneurs go through the world continuously seeking ideas and opportunities to commercialize. They focus on innovating, doing other things better, adding, creating and delivering unique value to customers and to all stakeholders, and they want to be rewarded for their successes. The more value they add, the greater their financial rewards. What I'm saying is you are rewarded in life by what you create as value for someone else. There is a reason why I chose to share my personal story with you in this chapter. I did it to show you that after you have decided that you want to create *REBELLIOU$ WEALTH*, your first decision is to choose your niche.

According to the Merriam Webster online dictionary, a niche is a place, employment status or activity for which a person or thing is best fitted or a specialized market. I make my living by helping people become self-reliant and getting what they want. To do this, I help them unlearn old behavior models and break free from learned helplessness.

My crime was wanting to feel powerful and in control. After creating my own little books and selling them through the mail, I created my own personal revolution. After reading damn near every book ever published on wealth and success, the information I obtained wasn't feeding me. I found that it only frustrated me. I wasn't fulfilled. I was supposed to accept what was being given to me, but I couldn't. A light went on in my head and I found the solution to my problem by recognizing that there are millions of others just like me who want to be rich but don't know how, who are also frustrated by information that's not feeding them. So, the key to my own success is to share what I have learned, provide a different kind of education and be a different kind of role model. This Made me feel powerful and in control and I developed a self-worth that's untouchable.

BIG STRONG
AND RESPECTED

I have learned a thing or two about people who accomplish great things. They never see themselves as great. When people tell me that they appreciate my books, it's amazing to me that anyone believes that they are special. I don't see it. I am nothing special. I just realized that any success that I wanted, I would have to go get it because no one was coming to save me. The really great make you feel that you can become great too, so your job as a *REBELLIOU$ WEALTH* seeker aka a bad boy or bad girl who finishes rich is to make what you are selling something that the other person wants. My preference is for you to read this entire book and extract from it ideas you act on and derive benefit from, but some of my clients agonize over finding their niche. I think it's important to find a niche that you are passionate about. As you know I am passionate about self-reliance and freedom. If that's your passion too, I think that if you follow the following guidelines, finding your niche becomes a nonproblem. Imagine the life you want and decide to live it! Devote your energy and lifeblood to its attainment! Set clear goals and a timetable for their completion! Never quit in the pursuit of your goals and see possibilities where others see problems! Always remember, rules are made for those who will follow them and until you are free economically, true independence is an afterthought!

Deep down, you may want to be in self-reliant, but there are real and perceived obstacles and risks. Remember, *REBELLIOU$ WEALTH* is a trial-and-error activity; the more times you try, the more you learn and the better you get at rebounding. You need to overcome fears and self-doubt about where the money will come from and stop being afraid to take all the risks required to get there. Fear of failure is a great motivator, especially if it's linked to survival then thriving. You need to find a subject that (1) you're passionate about, (2) you're knowledgeable in and (3) is broad enough to have a large customer base. My solution is to promote seminars, create videos, record audios and write books that teach people to create self-reliance, freedom and multiple streams of income. How much faith and follow through are you willing to give to launching your own Information business and creating *REBELIOU$ WEALTH*? You need less talent, skill, industry knowledge, money and other resources than you may believe because you can outsource most functions. Marshall Sylver said it best when he said, "Real estate won't make you wealthy, the Internet doesn't print cash and the stock market can't make you rich. You make you rich; more specifically, your habits make you rich. There's no way around it: your habits either make you or break you. You will either have discipline or regrets." So ask yourself, what type of person do I want to be? What type of lifestyle do I want? What big things do I want to accomplish in my life? What toys would I like to have for myself and my family and what kind of money do I want to make?

Most of us spend our lives as if we had another life to draw on in the future when this one runs out. Unfortunately the clock is always running. It's up to you to make sure that you don't waste your life away. You must make time work for you not against you. Live your life according to the motto *"REBELLIOU$ WEALTH!"* The key is to forget about what the masses are doing. You must take control of your physical and psychic space instead of allowing the distractions of the modern world to influence your lifestyle. To quote Douglas Everett, "There are some people who live in a dream world and there are some who face reality; and then there are those who turn one into the other." So ask yourself, what needs can you meet? Who looks to you as a leader? What bothers you about the world? How can you make things better? And what can you offer the world that no one else can?

When I am creating I feel like an athlete in the zone: powerful, relaxed and efficient because I am creating my own value and my own worth. Most importantly, I am controlling my own destiny. You must create new systems for success and eliminate those that are holding you back. Remember, every problem is a product. Find the problem and sell the solution.

"REBELLIOU$ WEALTH" – EXERCISE APPENDIX-B

Take a piece of paper and draw a line down the middle. On one side, write down all the subjects you're knowledgeable about. Take some time with this because you know more than you think you do. In the second column, make a similar list of things that you are passionate about. Take a look at your list and see what subject shows up in both columns then do a web search to see who is marketing to your future customers. If your search turns up page after page of commercial sites, congratulations! You just found your niche.

REBELLIOU$ WEALTH!

"I must create a system or be enslaved by another man's. I will not reason and compare; my business is to create."

~ William Blake

Chapter Three

THE AMERICAN DREAM...A LOVE STORY

(Write, direct, produce and star in your own path to wealth)

The starting point to all growth and development rests with a decision and the decision that you make can alter the course of your life forever. In *BAD BOYS FINISH RICH*, I offered the following advice: *"DON'T FIND A JOB, CREATE ONE!"* Each of us is the architect of our own fate, but we must lay the bricks ourselves. Life has taught me a deep respect not just for money but also for the game of money so I wanted to have control of my assets rather than just turn my career and my money over to strangers. My personal concern is that there are millions of people today who are working hard but losing the game. The main reason for this is a lack of understanding of our capitalistic system of government. Capitalism is defined as an economic system in which capital and capitalists play the principal part. Specifically, the established economic system of most modern civilized countries in which the ownership of land and natural wealth, the production, distribution, and exchange of goods, the employment and reward of human labor, and the extension, organization, and operation of the system itself, are entrusted to and effected by private enterprise and control, under competitive conditions. Since our capitalistic system is a competitive system, you must learn to compete with your fellowman. You must not only seek jobs, but you must own businesses that will give jobs to others. It's about taking control of your own financial future and it's about you learning to play your own game of money instead of giving your money to someone else and letting them play the game for you. A job is only a short term solution to the long term problem of how to survive financially, especially when you are not working or are unable to work any longer or lose everything and have to start all over again.

So what motivates you? Why did you pick up this book? How do you feel about what you've read so far? The purpose of our time together is to transform your thinking about life and work. It's not just about chasing the almighty buck for me. It's about growing my livelihood and creating services and things of value for other people. I know what you are thinking... You want to be in my position, not just my customer! Life is about transitioning from who we are right now into someone greater, someone better. I want you to reach for everything you can reach for. You don't understand the power that you have. In the mirror is the person who will become your mentor. They are filled with financial intelligence and their point of view represents the other side of entrepreneurship and money; the elite group that you want to belong to. It's just a rational response to the reality you face. As many of you know from reading *BAD BOYS FINI$H RICH*, my dad's death just kind of changed everything for me and I met the man who would become my mentor in the mirror. My mentor, the man in the mirror was an incredible man who taught me so much about having the will to fight. He took a fatherly interest in me, often telling me I should create my own products and go into business for myself. He became kind of a private tutor, teaching me business and finance. We spent hours talking and he'd give me examples until he was sure I understood it all. He encouraged me all the time. Initially, I was reluctant to accept his ideas, but I propelled my thoughts to an elevated state. That encouragement was very important. I already believed in myself and had confidence, but he made me feel that my confidence was justified. The more I thought about it, the more realistic the ideas became. My value would be what I created. I would live by my own judgment. I would accept no limits and I would refuse to accept inferiority. I would not live a contained, restricted or limited life. I would think outside of the box. I would be imaginative and creative and I would be adamant about navigating my own course.

Every man has to make his own footprints in the sand. I was the navigator of my own destiny. Despite being ridiculed for being different, my desire to transcend the world's expectations did not falter. Could it be done? I hoped so. In fact, I was beyond hope. I was certain. It was just a matter of time. Your strength is no more than an attitude you have about yourself. I am a different man now with a different mind-set. I see life differently. When he told me that I should create my own products, I believed him. I was struck by his power and charisma. The dream of being someone, of making my mark in the world burned hotter in me than ever, so I pushed myself harder. This has changed my life forever and it allowed me to reach my full potential and discover the real me.

THE BEST WAY TO CREATE
WEALTH EVER INVENTED

Information has always been the most important thing to me. I always learned by looking and listening. Although I knew it was time to live free, be free, create and go into business, there is always the insistent, insidious voice of skepticism. I didn't know a thing about creating my own products. How am I going to teach others a game that I haven't fully learned how to play? Why do I always think of these crazy ideas? To have contradictions, especially when you're fighting for your life is human. Feelings of doubt rocked me, but I had always been a dreamer, obsessed with originality, so why was this any different? It's easier to ask for forgiveness than permission and I don't need anyone's permission. Eliminating the last doubts from my mind, I studied every aspect of the Information business and today, I'm a businessman with legitimate products to promote and I'm not going to back down. Empowered by this knowledge, my lesson from this experience is a sound business strategy that anybody can learn from and imitate and it can be a direct path to creating your own economy.

As a *REBELLIOU$ WEALTH* seeker your advice, strategies for success and how-to knowledge can be packaged into informational products and programs that people purchase online. Your content can be offered through webinars, software, membership sites, downloadable audio and video programs, monthly content releases, desktop training programs and much,

much more. You can also promote seminars, create videos, record audios and write e-books that teach people to create multiple streams of passive income. An information program is often a book, e-book, CD audio program, or DVD home study course. An e-book is a PDF file that your customer can download from the Internet. This is how you make one: After you've done your research, write down the solution in the form of an article or short book. You can make it longer, but about thirty pages is a good length for a short e-book. After you have written it, convert it into a PDF file. You can do this by using a PDF converter such as: PDF Converter: freepdfconvert.com, PrimoPDF: primopdf.com, PDF Online: pdfonline.com/convert-pdf and Adobe Acrobat: adobe.com/products/acrobat/convert-pdf-converter.html. Some are free and some require membership, but these are a few examples that you can use to create your e-book and allow anybody who can access the internet to download it. There are other "create PDF ebook shareware" programs available but look for the software that's best for you.

Now, let's look at audio programs. Audio programs are easy to create. You just buy a decent microphone and plug it into your computer. With free software from your computer or software that you feel meets the quality that you want from the Internet, you can record your voice and training. A couple of easy to use audio programs are: Audacity audacity.sourceforge.net and WavePad Audio Editor: nch.com.au/software/audio.html. Once you have the MP3 files from your recordings, you can make them downloadable or send them to a CD manufacturer and have them create CD's and product design for you. Here are a few sources for DVD & CD replication, DVD & CD duplication and distribution. Oasis Disc Manufacturing: oasiscd.com, Bison Disc: bisondisc.com and Disc Makers: discmakers.com. It's that simple, now you have a product that the manufacturer prints on demand and fulfills for you.

Videos have a higher perceived value than audios and e-books. There are several ways to deliver video. The most common are Flash, QuickTime and Windows media. Any consumer video camera will get the job done and some come with editing software. You can use screen capture software such as Snagit: techsmith.com/snagit.html, Debut Video Capture Software: nchsoftware.com/capture/index.html or presentation software, such as PowerPoint: office.microsoft.com/en-us/powerpoint, Impress: openoffice.us.com or Keynote: apple.com/iwork/keynote. You can also use animation software such as Adobe Flash: dobe.com/products/flash.html or Microsoft Silverlight: microsoft.com/silverlight to clearly outline the advantages and important aspects of the product. Use video editing software such as Power Director: cyberlink.com, Corel VideoStudio Pro X6: corel.com or Adobe Premiere Elements 11: adobe.com/products/premiere-elements.html to combine the various aspects of your video together into a smooth presentation. If you enjoy delivering your solutions in video format, you might want to invest in better cameras and editing software. In conclusion, the proven *REBELLIOU$ WEALTH* system is to sell downloadable digital files that are delivered instantly and automatically through the internet.

FIGHTING FOR SUCCESS LIKE A TRUE CHAMPION

By comparison, I had nothing. I was just living life, trying to get through, survive, thrive, whatever, but in the back of my mind, there was always a larger plan that I was trying to make sense of. The consensus was, this is the way it's supposed to be and the way it will always be. Maybe it was supposed to be that way for them, but I thought I had a better way. They were climbing the same hill, the same way. I decided to climb my own hill. Every now and then God sends somebody to show the world that everything is possible with him. My mentor, the man in the mirror, believed in me and helped me reach a better level. Creating my own products gave me a feeling of accomplishment like none I had ever had. Today I am a pioneer on the frontier staking out new territory where I can run things myself. I never want to give that up to become someone's contracted employee. Your dreams and big ideas belong to no one but you and you never have to apologize for or justify them to anyone. Let you imagination go crazy. It doesn't cost a thing to come up with a great idea. *REBELLIOU$ WEALTH* seekers place their ideas and creations before a crowd; the others stand in the crowd and look. We may fear risk but take it anyway and risk everything to find success, not only for ourselves, but for our kids, our families, even our communities. Critics will try to burst your bubble and interfere with your plans even when they don't have a direct interest in them. Somebody somewhere will find a reason to complain, but carry yourself with strength and confidence. You need to be in control of your own financial decisions and not give that power to someone else. What makes your product unique and valuable is that you'll be telling your story and providing your solution to a problem in your own voice.

The key to success begins by committing yourself to an inspiring cause that impacts others in a positive way and believing in the quality of your own product enough to make people do business with you on your terms. There were many bouts and devastating rounds, but I kept punching until I was able to get off the ropes. Tear away the pessimism, the cowardice, and the status quo state of mind. If you want to walk amongst *BAD BOYS who FINI$H RICH*, you must alter your habits, refine your thinking, embrace the unlimited possibilities that lie within your reach, take control of your life and keep your eyes on the prize.

"REBELLIOU$ WEALTH" – EXERCISE APPENDIX-C

Your thoughts and ideas can turn into products and your product is a solution to your customer's problem. You're looking for problems that cause a lot of pain for a large group of people and that pain is going to help you create your own economy.

Surf through social media and take note of what problems your friends are talking about. Take a piece of paper and draw a line down the middle. On one side, write down the most common problems. In the second column, make a similar list of what problem is causing them the most pain. Take a look at your list and see which problems you can solve quickly and turn that problem into your into your product.

REBELLIOU$ WEALTH!

"Donald Trump was in New York saying that's my building, that's my Bank, that's my Hotel and I'm like oh, I ain't made it yet. I could go that's my watch, that's my car, that's my house, that's my car, but I wasn't saying that's my Bank, that's my building. You know, that's a whole different game. That's what brought me to the game to say you know what, it ain't bout the bling. When I woke up and understood that, I am the most dangerous man in hip hop now."

~ Master P

Chapter Four

CEO STATUS DESPITE THE LACK
OF AN ADVANCED DEGREE

(There is a big difference between being in charge and being in control)

Most people spend a lot of money buying everything but don't own anything. Reiterating my question from BAD BOYS FINI$H RICH, "Where is your power if you are still just an employee or a customer of a business owned by someone else?" If you want REBELLIOU$ WEALTH, you have to embrace economic freedom, and with the mind-set of ownership, you will begin to have more control over your destiny. The choice of an unremarkably average life represents a life of sleepwalking. To break out of the sleepwalking pattern, we have to define what we want and then find a way to make it happen.

As I searched for my own economic freedom, I felt like something was missing and as I shared with you earlier, I wasn't fulfilled. I wasn't sure what I was looking for, but I knew it was out there somewhere. Sometimes I even felt hopeless and hopelessness is a heavy weight on your shoulders; sometimes too heavy to carry. Enough was enough. I couldn't take it anymore. Not one more day. I decided that I would create my own game within the game and always be an owner by creating my own intellectual property, enabling me to spread my personal philosophy, message and principles of self-reliance. I would introduce a new generation of players. That was my idea. That was the plan. My readers would inherit my knowledge and take the world by storm. Like going to Wall Street where bankers do business. Instead of stocks and bonds, I would push Information. But the decision to introduce the *BAD BOYS FINI$H RICH* and *REBELLIOU$ WEALTH* principles to the world and create a new breed of rich people required planning that was outside the bounds of my experience. Were these the thoughts of a rational man? Where would I start? Who would I get to help me? I had no way to begin except to pick up my computer and begin to play my own game.

ENTREPRENEURSHIP IN PRACTICE NOT THEORY

I have a genuine heart-felt desire to empower people, to raise them to a higher level of existence, but the hardest thing about fulfilling this desire is knowing where to start. Maybe you've encountered this same challenge. My objective was to provide key principles which I believe are essential to bringing about positive change and the best possible good for others. I have never regretted my decision for an instant because there is nothing like the feeling of having earned something as opposed to having it given to you and I had a story to tell. I was going forth to live my own life with faith and courage and I had faith that my way was right and the confidence to back it up. You gain all the confidence in the world when you believe and I knew that if I just continued, I would never be inferior or subservient to anyone in any way ever again. I had expectations that I wanted to live up to. From now on, it didn't matter anymore. I'd be the first to win. I had my theories and yes, you can't know if a theory is correct until you test it. But none of this is coincidence, so let me show you a cold, calculated plan to provide a valuable service, make money and create your own economy:

1. Once you choose your subject, package your training material, advice and strategies for success into a low-priced educational product or program typically in the price range of $20-$200.

2. Create a low-priced subscription program: Deliver content to your customers in a continuity program or membership program just like the magazine business model by sending monthly content to them in

the form of a training video or by hosting a training call over a conference call line which gives them more training or answers questions. To access the video and the call replays, your customers will login to a members-only site and download the video or audio recordings.

You can do this by using subscription or membership programs such as: paymentonline.com, memberclicks.com and amember.com

3. Create a mid-tier-priced information product: A more advanced and comprehensive training program such as a $497 DVD home study course on your topic. The home study course could include 10 DVDs, transcripts, a workbook and a bonus 3-disc audio program.

   Here's how to quickly put together the perfect script for your next how-to video or DVD. Follow the basic time line template located in the appendix section of your study guide. Stick to these guidelines and you'll be able to create the kind of production your customers will value.

4. Create a high-tier multi-day seminar: Customers are interested in mastery and continuing their education. If they bought your book, audio and DVD programs, now they want to go deeper and learn from you live.

Let me give you a quick lesson on creating a seminar: First choose your topic for your presentation based on the needs of your target audience. Choose your presentation format. Do you want to do a workshop which is hands-on with your participants or do you want to do a seminar where your audience participates less? Based on the amount of material you want to communicate to your audience, you'll need to establish the length of your presentation and create an outline for the flow of your presentation. Next you'll need to select visual aids for your presentation such a flip chart, PowerPoint presentation or a video depending on your topic. And finally, you'll want to practice your presentation on a test group that's willing to provide you with feedback. Just as with your video, these general guidelines will allow you to be able to create the kind of presentation your customers will value.

5. Create a high-priced coaching program: Customers want your personal attention. They want you to assess their needs and work with them to develop a plan to move them closer towards their dream.

    Here's a broad overview on creating a coaching program: First choose your topic for your coaching program based on the needs of your target audience. Next, decide if you want to do individual or group coaching. Then, as you did with developing your video script, develop the curriculum that supports your subject and provide exclusive training every month with question and answer sessions. With your coaching program, the value that your customer will get is the exclusive access to you.

Now of course, that alone doesn't make you successful. There's more to the equation. Look for the believability that there's a problem that needs to be solved in the marketplace and that that problem can be solved by you. You should also address and understand what you don't know. Remember, the result you get from any situation depends largely on the thought you put into it. Do nothing and you'll get nothing. It's just that simple. It isn't knowledge that has power, it's the use of knowledge and it isn't what you learn that guarantees success; it's actually what you do. I also encourage people to tell their own stories and I encourage you to tell your story because life is not a game, it's a reality show and every episode is a learning experience. To quote JaRule, "I'm going to show the world my struggle, my pain, my hunger, my hustle!" It will surely help someone else and it will help you.

As you can see, this is a complete do-it-yourself approach, but there are a lot of services out there to help you get started. So invest your time in the *REBELLIOUS WEALTH* system that you're most comfortable with. As a *REBELLIOUS WEALTH* seeker, what's so important about the work that we do? The answer is simple: We all want to make a difference in the world and most important, we all recognize challenges as opportunities waiting to happen. People want to be a part of a real and meaningful mission. Your job as a *REBELLIOU$ WEALTH* seeker is to create the opportunity for them to be rebellious. The value of the endgame needs to be what matters to you and your intended audience because perception is reality, right?

YOU MUST BE CONFUSED I
DON'T NEED YOUR PERMISSION

When I made up my mind about something, there was no stopping me. My laid back persona, million dollar smile and unique talent are a powerhouse not to be fucked with. Great products tell a story under the surface. They connect the dots and they work deep into the subconscious. My identity of not being a team player determined who I could become and what opportunities I could enjoy. The products are simply the means to a more important end. I am building leaders and I am sharing my vision and developing a philosophy of commitment and a culture of self-sufficiency. This is the place where non team players can be who they are and still be treated with respect. *REBELLIOU$ WEALTH* gives you confidence. It is the inner strength that lets you believe in yourself and a positive outcome. It is the lack of fear of your competitors. It is the strength to seize the moment and play without fear. It is the depth inside you that you draw from to find peace and it is the certainty that you will win. You've got to believe that you can do it with "Singleness of Purpose." Anything is possible with the right method. We must learn to take what you have and make what you want to manufacture and participate in business. I place emphasis on the fact that you should develop an economic base and participate in every aspect of commerce that controls your life because where there is security there can be no freedom. I know if I had to depend on others all my life to furnish me with work I wouldn't have made the progress I needed to make to get what I wanted from life. The only thing standing in my way was my attitude and I had a spark of ambition under the surface, dying to get out.

I came to realize that I had to cross an invisible line by switching up the same old formula and adding other elements. I had to go outside the boundary lines. I was going to push the envelope. Here is when I realized that I am me; A Bad Boy, Rebellious and Bad Ass. It was something that was in me that I could claim as my own and it is important to make sure that my individual creative rights are protected. I'm an artist and I had to express myself as an artist. *REBELLIOU$ WEALTH* is all about fearlessness and attitude and I'm not just selling information, I am creating culture. Not too many people devote time to think about their purpose in life. They just coast along, taking life as it comes. That's what I had done. But if you are motivated to make a difference in the world, then you regularly take a few minutes to think about where you are headed. How grateful for life can you be if all you do is get up in the morning, go to work, come home, eat dinner, watch TV and then go to bed? What purpose are you serving? What goals are you achieving? It takes no initiative, no courage and no wisdom to consume what other men produce. Somebody has to show you that you can gain *REBELLIOU$ WEALTH* by taking something into the relationship, not just taking everything out of it. I look at it this way, "I know what you gain if you're with me, what do I gain if I'm with you?" *REBELLIOU$ WEALTH* demands commitment, perseverance, stamina, strength, power, control, patience, tolerance and focus because a commitment is really a challenge; and if you make the commitment, you must follow through because your commitment is you. Knowledge is power, power that controls and demands, and power is the ability to win. Regardless of where we are, the time is always right for each of us to say and do something that will make a difference in the world. Your ambition and your aspiration are proof of your ability to reach your dream and the only inferiority in you is that which you place on yourself. This is your chance to rise to you greatest self because you are in control of your creativity.

"REBELLIOU$ WEALTH" – EXERCISE APPENDIX-D

This is a test of whether you can create your own economy. You have to know yourself well to make the right decision. Take your time. The key is to use a rational decision-making process that gives consideration to your dreams. Getting started may not be easy but there is a lot of help available to accomplish anything that you want to accomplish. You just need to find it.

- Are you willing to make personal sacrifices today in exchange for undetermined rewards in the future?

- Are you willing to trust your decisions when others aren't?

- Are you willing to take risks?

- Are you willing to accept rejection?

- Are you willing to use your creativity and be more innovative than the average person?

- Are you willing to experience a lot of failure and learn from it, before experiencing a lot of success?

- Are you willing to do a lot of research?

- Are you willing to adopt the success principles of successful people?

- Are you willing to get paid for the actual results you produce instead of for the time you spend at a job?

- Are you willing to forego a regular paycheck and get paid sporadically sometimes a little, sometimes a lot?

The bottom line is if you can tolerate risk and uncertainty, cope well with failure while you are learning the ropes and work creatively and independently, then *REBELLIOU$ WEALTH* is for you. The key is to give a lot of thought to the lifestyle you would like and what you want to achieve.

REBELLIOU$ WEALTH!

"I'm different; yea I'm different!"

~ 2 Chains

Chapter Five

THE LAST MAN STANDING

(How do you get to be great? You make yourself think that you are great)

The word rebellious has an ugly implication, but a strong sense of self both internally and externally is the engine that powers who you are. When you are standing in front of a mirror, all you can see is you, so you need to dig deep into your flesh and bones to discover this core sense of self and then you must own it. That's what *REEBLLIOU$ WEALTH* does. It forces us to connect the dots between our inside and the outside. You need to have a strong sense of self because without it there's no distinction between you and everybody else. When you do something that you know is rebellious, embrace it, run with it and trust yourself. Was this attitude placed in you simply to be killed? Never! I know some people love to look down on you and say something dismissive but that's not my opinion. You've got a world of discovery and a few rude awakenings ahead and questions of who you are and why you are here are extremely important. This is the season for exploration, transformation and discovering who we are and what our place in the world might be. Our dreams and desires need to awaken, grow and mature and we need to awaken, grow and mature so that we might be able to handle these dreams and desires.

REBELLIOU$ WEALTH is all about revolution. It is a revolution to its core. You are taking this course so that you might discover both the joy of being a part of this revolution and find your own unique place within it. Some people feel that life should be easy, dreams should come true and everybody should get a prize no matter how they perform. Those people are truly shocked when they come to realize, often painfully, that the world doesn't owe them a thing, which leaves them trapped in an endless journey. Well, the journey is one thing, but the destination is a completely different animal and my job is to give you hope to begin the journey. Yes, of course you have a journey before you, but it has a destination. And that destination is possessing an attitude and strength that allows you to be self-reliant and free. I'm honest with myself about my own transformation from slave to freedom. Second guessing every move feels like a recipe for going nowhere and I don't want to go nowhere. I want meaning and purpose. I want to know that I am stepping into something that matters and that it's something worth doing. For the most part, I love my life and you can find a life that you love, but I didn't just step into this position. *REBELLIOU$ WEALTH* starts with a dream and the dedication and commitment to make that dream come true. There was a lot that had to happen in me before I could live the life I live now and I came to realize that these were the ideas that mattered most.

THE ULTIMATE SIGN OF REBELLION

✓ REBELLIOU$ WEALTH seekers are dream catchers. They catch their dreams by any means necessary and follow them through!

✓ REBELLIOU$ WEALTH seekers are true warriors. They are so driven by determination that they will stop at nothing to succeed!

✓ REBELLIOU$ WEALTH seekers are confident that they will be the victor. They are focused on the prize and no matter how tough the challenge, they will rise to it!

✓ REBELLIOU$ WEALTH seekers treasure their unique gift. Whatever it is that has been bestowed upon them by God!

✓ REBELLIOU$ WEALTH seekers don't understand the concept of being mediocre or second best!

✓ REBELLIOU$ WEALTH seekers treasure life and live it abundantly and to the fullest!

✓ REBELLIOU$ WEALTH seekers set life goals to make something out of nothing!

✓ REBELLIOU$ WEALTH seekers keep on going even when they are laughed at and belittled!

✓ REBELLIOU$ WEALTH seekers go on even when everyone turns against them, doesn't understand and leaves them standing alone!

✓ REBELLIOU$ WEALTH seekers go one more step while the next person falls short.
✓ REBELLIOU$ WEALTH seekers put their trust in what's right and come out victorious; and even if they don't, they take it in stride.

When you have *REBELLIOUS WEALTH*, you have confidence in all you do. You're happy with what you do, what you say, the way you look and the way you conduct yourself. It's not an accident. It's a deliberate attempt to succeed.

THE EXTRAORDINARY FEAT OF FUNCTIONING SUCCESSFULLY IN A MODERN SOCIETY

Deep in our marrow lies a passion to be a part of something BIG. The choice before you is a bold one: to accept the wild daring process of becoming rebellious. The beauty of accepting the process releases you from the pressure of following the crowd. The plot really is that simple at its essence. You are in the thick of exploring who you are, what you are and why you are here and *REBELLIOU$ WEALTH* seekers want something higher, greater, so they accept the process. I always wanted to get from A to B as fast as possible and keep it moving. I never felt that other people's ways were fast enough for me. I couldn't stand just being told something. I wanted to get out there and find out for myself, but it takes courage and perseverance. It takes a warrior.

I am not afraid to dream and yearn for everything that I would like to see happen in my life so the result is a course about moving in the direction of your dreams, wrestling through doubt and setbacks and in the end your dream can be realized. I love this story because it evolved from the research to the writing stage and it was erected upon uncompromising idealism and policies pursued with vigor. I believe that if I move in the direction of my dreams and fight my way through setbacks, my life will be full of adventure and I will find treasure. I'm able to let my dreams run wild and I have a profound joy of knowing I'm having an impact on the world. But some people aren't able to let their dreams run wild. As time passes, a mysterious force begins to convince them that it will be impossible for them to realize their dreams. According to Melchizedek, they believe the world's greatest lie. What's the world's greatest lie? "It's this: that at a certain point in our lives, we lose control of what's happening to us and our lives become controlled by fate. That's the world's greatest lie." Let me offer a piece of wisdom: we are afraid of losing what we have, whether it's our life or our possessions and property. But this fear evaporates when we understand that our life stories and the history of the world were written by *REBELLIOUS WEALTH* seekers like you and me. People want what other people seem to be enjoying and this course is speaking deep truth to you. It is whispering a promise that you yearn to hear: "It can be done. Life can work out. Dreams do come true." I know what they say about me. That I am cocky, don't follow orders and not a team player. Not the one you'd expect to be the last man standing once the smoke has cleared. Yet here I am, in the position to tell my story. If you are outside the story, living in a great story looks and feels quite different than watching one unfold. I had to forge a new business model. Compared to others, I was always the out-spoken, brash, cocky person in the room. Not as cooperative or unassuming as some. This would appear in some ways to make me the least likely to succeed. But the thing about being rebellious is that you most likely have a greater capacity to win. All of these rebellious qualities turned out to be the very virtues that contributed to me winning at my own game.

The story of *REBELLIOUS WEALTH* is in many ways the story of the ability to strike a note of empathy and recognition in people who think like me, act like me, dream like me, have the same longings and aspirations and have experienced the same pains and disappointments. The very definition on which to lay all the hopes, aspirations, wishes, desires and even fantasies of a group of people long denied affirmation. So this course is directed at any person who wants to figure out how to play what's often thought of as "THE MAN'S game and win. Again, it's not about whether you can or you can't, it's about whether you will or you won't. *REBELLIOUS WEALTH* is like a car. It can take you to good places; it can take you to bad places. It can open up adventures and it can do some serious damage. Everything depends on who's driving. Attitude, courage and perseverance, that's how you create *REBELLIOUS WEALTH*. Live that and you will have a story worth telling.

"REBELLIOUS WEALTH" – EXERCISE APPENDIX-E

Ownership and playing your own game within the game can come in the form of positioning yourself as an expert within your niche. Rise to the challenge by defining your *REBELLIOUS WEALTH* purpose, mission, vision and story and aligning them with your products and your brand.

- What is your *REBELLIOUS WEALTH* purpose, mission and vision? (A clear definition of your purpose, mission and vision is critical to both the joy of achieving what you set out to do and your own unique place within it.)

- What is your *REBELLIOUS WEALTH* story? (Once you have defined your purpose, mission, and vision you need to be able to align that with a story that you want to share.)

- How will you create a culture that is in alignment with your purpose, mission, vision and story? (Make your customers/followers/fans feel more aligned with your company purpose, mission and vision.)

- What strategies will you use to tell your story effectively? (Social media, your own events)

REBELLIOU$ WEALTH!

"Like we always do at this time, I go for mine, I got to shine. Welcome to the good life!"

~ *Kanye West*

Chapter Six

THE SUCCESSFUL, THE POWERFUL,
THE ACCOPLISHED

(A chance to rise to your greatest self)

All entrepreneurs share similar qualities. We possess an inner desire to create something of value for others and achieve something bigger than life. And when we follow our desire we have the potential to achieve the unimaginable by simply being tenacious enough to take the first step and follow through on our vision. That tenacity and dedication can lead to fulfilling desires that are beyond your wildest dreams. That's what's happening with *REBELLIOUS WEALTH*. Every great success is the result of hundreds and even thousands of little efforts that no one ever sees or appreciates, so I have messed up millions of times to bring you this body of work. More importantly, I have poured my heart and soul into it. We've come a long way and I hope that I have fulfilled your *REBELLIOUS WEALTH* mission and I hope I have inspired and instructed you on how you can improve your life. You can make a real career as an Information entrepreneur and create your own economy if you simply position, package, promote and partner with others to get your message out there. You can do this. Now is your time. Sharing your message will be a meaningful act and a true path to your purpose and fulfillment in life. You can focus solely on selling your information product as an e-book, audio program or DVD or building a monthly subscription/membership program. Or you can sell your more advanced, comprehensive training program, conduct seminars or provide individual or group coaching. It doesn't require you to have dozens of products or thousands of clients. You just need a few programs for your customers to enroll in. Of course this is just a sample plan. Depending on the income you desire and the commitment that you make to building your business there are plenty of ways to reach millions more.

We all have different levels of ambition, knowledge, skill, talent, ability, resources and commitment so we are all going to get different results. My goal in illustrating this simple plan is to show you how just a few product offerings can add up to a big opportunity so that it is no longer a mystery to you. Information is the most powerful force on earth. That is why the control of information is essential to the control of power. Why? Because the lack of information enslaves billions of people. Now more than ever, millions of people are looking for something unique and of particular and precise relevance to them and are willing to pay premium prices or fees for it. They also want inspiration to help them get ahead and instruction to help them stay motivated. I know personally, being an avid reader and someone who likes to write and share ideas that I am very thankful that the Information business that I own allows me an opportunity to do what I have done on my own terms. I learned that not only was I in the Information business, but even more so in the business of the dissemination of ideas. While there is a large demand for information, there is an even greater demand for ideas.

THE BALLS TO CHASE YOUR DREAMS: LIKE BEING BORN INTO A RICH AND POWERFUL FAMILY

Most people go their entire lives and never find something that captures their interest to the extent that they'll spend almost every waking moment strategizing about it. Have you ever really wanted something so bad that you were willing to do whatever it took to get it? Well that's what I felt about being self-reliant. *REBELLIOUS WEALTH* seekers are able to channel a very large majority if not all of their energies into one endeavor until it is successfully completed. However, many people are defeated in the pursuit of their dream from the very beginning because they have convinced themselves that it can't be achieved. On the other hand, some people dream too much and your self-reliance requires more than just dreams. It requires an alteration in lifestyle. This course was designed to build personal wealth because the world needs *REBELLIOU$ WEALTH* seekers that are economically knowledgeable and committed to the overall development of self-reliance; showing non-team players that they can be anything and everything they want to be. *REBELLIOU$ WEALTH* seekers are risk takers and have high self-esteem. Most people who have moderate or low self-esteem play by the rules and are very concerned about what other people would think of their failure. Consequently, their own personal goals, desires and dreams are seldom fulfilled because they are afraid of taking a risk. Your self-esteem would be low too, if your life wasn't in your hands and if you had no potential to improve your quality of life.

Now I am in no way endorsing anyone to act as a gambler and role the dice. What I am saying is that *REBELLIOU$ WEALTH* seekers should think differently about wealth and success and self-imposed limitations. This requires a greater understanding and acceptance of who you really are. If that sounds cocky, you wouldn't be the first person to think it. I'm simply trying to get you to be true to yourself. Consequently, I'm not offering you a fool proof blueprint. My path wasn't exactly mistake-free and a straight line to success. My objective is not that you emulate my path, but that I help you find your own path. My blueprint will provide a range of options and pathways that can lead you to the same destination of learning, playing, mastering and creating your own game within the game, your way. The reality of *REBELLIOU$ WEALTH* is a lot harder than anyone who hasn't been through it could know. It can be the most frustrating, tedious, crazy, exhausting, exhilarating, beautiful and rewarding life for anyone who can stand the heat. Unfortunately, the people who are short term oriented do not envision processing this information into personal wealth and transferring that wealth to their children. Since very few people are going to inherit a million dollars, we should concentrate our efforts on *REBELLIOU$ WEALTH*.

DOING WHAT CAN'T BE
DONE IS THE GLORY OF LIVING

Most people have been made aware of certain strategies that can be used to generate wealth, but choose not to make a decision. No decision is a decision not to grow and develop. Another reason is attitude and one component of attitude that hinders wealth is not being able to think big. Many people simply cannot comprehend *REBELLIOU$ WEALTH*. They're satisfied just making it and that term reflects what they think of themselves because many of us create our own limitations. An additional hindrance has been our desire for a guarantee. Many people are looking for a guarantee. They would prefer a guaranteed salary than a percentage of an unlimited amount of income. They would rather receive a lower guaranteed fixed rate of return than to potentially receive a higher rate of return without the guarantee, but very few people grow rich with all their money invested in a guaranteed source of income. It takes courage to step into the world of money and by avoiding it we lose the ability to play a larger role. But, let's take money off the table for a minute. What I'm trying to do here is get you to relax, to not be so preoccupied with getting, so you can focus on giving and creating products of value for others. The most beautiful thing of all is this: If we will align ourselves to the *REBELLIOU$ WEALTH* way of doing things, money will not rule our lives, nor will fear. Money won't even be what we are thinking about because we will be chasing higher things. People ask me how I even know what to do, but there are some things you can just figure out for yourself. At the end of the day, it doesn't matter, if you are the one with the blueprint, others have to follow. I know this is a challenging endeavor. Even more so, it's a journey of continuous learning and self-discovery. Things may not always blow up on the first try, but that's how you learn exactly what to do for the next time. Without the passion and the drive to succeed it's a very difficult task. I still have my moments of doubt, but I rarely think about it when I'm in the zone. It's rare that we get this kind of shot at the top of the entrepreneurship ladder and there's a built-in expectation that we won't make it, but it just drives us even harder to succeed. I'm not a person who has to do anything I don't want to do. My life is what it is. I'm content with being who I am.

For every *REBELLIOU$ WEALTH* seeker, there is that moment just before you jump off the cliff into the abyss of pure risk that you hesitate for just a second, give in to self-doubt and second–guessing for just a minute, then finally take a deep breath and go for it. There are people who will support and believe in you. There are people who will discourage and criticize you. Either way, you must have the strength to sustain your battle. As a *REBELLIOU$ WEALTH* seeker, you will have to fight to hang on to your dreams. Either you are your own greatest ally or you are completely on your own. What you believe about this affects everything else. There is an old quote that says, "All the world cries, where is the man or woman who will save us? Don't waste your time searching for this individual, for he or she is at hand. This man, this woman is you and me. This individual is each of us. You are the architect of your own future. Your fortune is not something to find but to unfold." Although I don't know you personally, I know a lot about you. You are smart, educated, articulate, hardworking, competitive, driven and full of energy, but at the same time, you are not exactly where you want to be and getting to that elusive next level is proving to be difficult. There's more to all of us than we realize. Life is much bigger, grander, higher and wider than we allow ourselves to think. We are capable of so much more than we allow ourselves to believe. As I have told you a trillion times, I believe in self-reliance. I believe in changing the things we have the ability to change and control. Each of us has the power to change ourselves. Successfully establishing a strong identity and purpose are part of a foundation that ultimately gives you the ability to forge ahead independently without being encumbered by society's expectations of who you are and what you can achieve. Knowing who you are in the context of your upbringing and the world around you allows you to learn and be the best at whatever you choose to pursue and puts you in a position to effectively play your game within the game.

To some of you, *REBELLIOU$ WEALTH* and all you have read is just a book and to a few, it points to the opportunity of a lifetime. You've got to understand that *REBELLIOUS WEALTH* is an unlimited idea of freedom. Only you can choose what will give you the most interesting challenge and satisfaction. The question is, will you continue to completely assimilate the values of popular culture or will you break the rules and challenge the norms to leverage your own game within the game? Personally, I am confidently charting a course that is different from the stereotypes, so I hope this course has affected you personally and emotionally because you can do it too. The formula is here. The methods are here. The ideas, tips, techniques, inspiration and motivation are all here. All you have to do is apply what I have taught you. Put in the work and you will get the results you want!

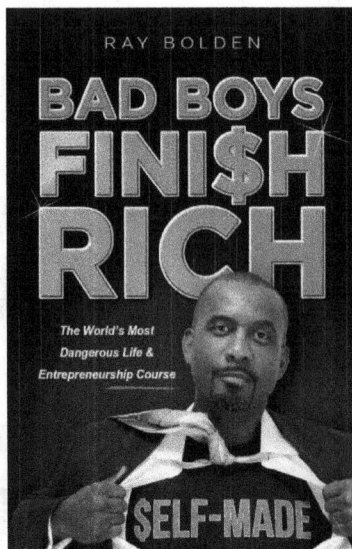

From RAY BOLDEN, Author of the Best Seller "BAD BOYS FINI$H RICH"

A BOOK FOR A VIDEO

BE A PART OF THE THOUSANDS OF LIVES CHANGED WITH THE HELP OF THE BAD BOYS FINI$H RICH PRINCIPLES!

Here's How It Works:

1. Once you receive your book, create a video of you holding up the book and enthusiastically saying the following:

I'm (First & Last Name) from (City & State or City and Country)!
"Bad Boys or Bad Girls" Finish Rich! (Based on your gender)
I Got My Copy, Get Yours!

2. Post the video on your Facebook page along with badboysfinishrich.com or your affiliate link.

3. Email the link of your video to admin@badboysfinishrich.com.

Once we receive your video link and verify it for clarity and authenticity, we will add it to our growing list of videos.

Please Note: Please follow the script provided above. We reserve the right to reject and refuse any videos deemed substandard or inappropriate.

Visit **BADBOYSFINISHRICH.COM/book4video**
for examples!

FOLLOW RAY ON SOCIAL MEDIA

PERSPECTIVES ON FINANCIAL LITERACY AND ENTREPRENEURIAL EDUCATION THAT OFTEN CONTRADICT CONVENTIONAL WISDOM

Follow Ray on Facebook:

www.facebook.com/boldambitionworldwide

Follow Ray on Twitter:

www.twitter.com/IamMrBolden

Follow Ray on Amazon:

www.amazon.com/Ray-Bolden/e/B00VXC3YN4/ref=ntt_dp_epwbk_0

Please Note: After enjoying Ray's work, please provide a customer review and give feedback on Amazon.com.

Visit **BADBOYSFINISHRICH.COM/about_ray**

BAD BOYS FINISH RICH

BOLD AMBITION
WORLDWIDE

www.ingramcontent.com/pod-product-compliance
Lightning Source LLC
Chambersburg PA
CBHW071120210326
41519CB00020B/6360